# Putting the Puzzle Together:
# A Modern Business Perspective

# Putting the Puzzle Together:
# A Modern Business Perspective

## Kaylin Hessler

Published by Kaylin Hessler
2018

First Printing: 2016

ISBN 978-1-365-53231-1

www.puttingthepuzzletogether.biz

# Dedication

To all small busness owners, good luck!

# Disclaimer

This book is one perspective of the business world. It should not take the place of legal or tax advice. Please seek the appropriate professional for your situation.

# Contents

# Acknowledgements

This book is for all the people who believed in me and helped in my business adventure.

## The Beginning

Everyone has an opinion and a different experience. This is only my version of what happened. Listen to everyone. They all have good points and can help you. However, step back and look at yourself and your customers and see if it makes sense. If it doesn't make sense for you and your business, don't do it.

People will also tell you, "This is how you start a business" or "This is just how things are done." That is crap. Every single business and every business owner is different. Otherwise, we would all have the same business and there would be no ingenuity. The purpose of your business is to be different. That way you will stand out and people will want to buy from you. The question is, how can we all be the same and different at the same time in a world today when there are so many new ways of doing things; new studies, apps, and solutions.

## Get A Mentor

Mentors can be amazing. If you can find a good one, hold on to them. They can change everything for you. The good ones are very hard to find. I stumbled upon mine at a networking event. He was a client of mine and asked me to do some work for him. Then he just started picking my brain and giving me advice. He is still a client of mine and one of my biggest proponents. We would be having a meeting about his business and he would stop and say, "putting on my coaching hat" and tell me everything I just did wrong. Mentors tend to be serial entrepreneurs and have been around the block. The key is that they see the vision for your business and can help you. Don't let a mentor make your business into theirs. That is not helpful.

## Learn to Listen

Listen to your customers. They will tell you what you need. Watch their face, see their reaction. Don't be afraid to adjust your product or your whole business for that matter. You are filling a need. Listen to their needs.

When I walked into my first big networking event thinking I knew exactly what I was going to do. I had the business plan, the sales pitch, and the product. I did everything that the books told me to do. Within 30 minutes of this daylong event, I realized that it wasn't going to work. I threw everything out the window! I shifted right there on the spot and never looked back.

Everywhere you look there is so much importance placed on the business plan. I agree it can be very important to organize yourself. I spent so much time on the business plan, but still changed everything in 30 minutes and never looked at it again. I kept thinking about all the time I wasted. I really only know a couple of people who have stuck by their business plan after writing it. I tried it. It was so much work; 58 pages long. Worthless.

Business plans can help you to organize yourself before you go on any venture, to make sure that it is what you want to do and how you are going to do it. But before you spend countless hours and spend money for templates or coaching or whatever, think about your business and your customers. If you need funding for your business, you will definitely need one. If you are doing this on your own, or with a partner, the business plan is only for you. If you need it to organize yourself or think that you will refer to it, go right ahead. Just know who and what it is for.

So now you have an idea, you read the books, you have a plan, where do you start?

# Starting

The first thing that you have to do is decide what type of business you want. There are many different structures for legal and tax reasons based on what you are trying to accomplish. It depends on what state you are in, and whether you have products or services. Are you the only owner? Who is going to run it? Will there be stock? These are questions you will have to answer. I highly suggest you talk to a lawyer to pick their brain. Later on, if you do want to change, you can. It might cost you, but you can change things. There are LLCs, Corporations, Sole Proprietorship. Each of these have their own legal and tax implications.

You will need to visit the IRS website and get an Employer Identification Number (EIN). Then you have to register with the state or town. Depending on your business, you may have to register for additional licenses, for example, sales tax or a liquor license.

## Sales Tax

Sales tax is collected from the end user of a physical product. As a business owner, it is your job to collect the sales tax. The customers pay for it, but you are a holder of the money for the state. If you are selling a service, there is no sales tax. The sales tax rules and rates vary from state to state.

Once all the legal paperwork is filled out, go to the bank and open up a new bank account for your business as soon as possible. Things can get very messy if you pay for items through your personal accounts or vice versa. It is hard to keep track of expenses, and this can be used against you in the legal world as "piercing the shield." Piercing the shield is what happens when personal and business assets are used interchangeably.

Depending on your legal business structure, you might have to legally separate yourself from the business. The benefit of this is that if the business is sued, they can only go after the assets in the business. If you "Pierce the Shield" then you and the business are essentially one and you can be sued for all your personal assets. Please consult a lawyer

Many banks will insist that you need a couple of different bank accounts. The most common is a Checking, Savings, Payroll, and or Operating Account. This separation is a very good idea, later. It works and is used in large companies for internal controls so not everyone has access to the money. However, that isn't always practical as a new small business owner. Most likely one or two people will have access to all the accounts, making this internal control useless. Personally, I have a Checking and Savings account. Simple.

Sometimes a Line of Credit will come with the banking package. If they offer you one, take it. Don't withdraw money from it until you need it. It is not free money! It is a loan.

What are your options for financing? Sometimes, banks aren't willing to lend without knowing if your venture will be successful enough to make good on your obligation. Entrepreneurs start their businesses with savings, put startup costs on credit cards or get loans from family and friends. The void in bank lending has spurred the growth of alternative lending, which can be costly, but gets money to entrepreneurs quickly and without a lot of hassle. One example of this is crowdfunding through websites such as Kickstarter and Indiegogo.

Some niche alternatives that have sprung up are not well known. For instance, culinary businesses can apply to the Whole Foods Local Producer loan program, which lends money to businesses making local food products. Many franchisers also help prospective franchisees with financing through a home equity loan, which was once a common source of startup cash.

Perhaps a more realistic option for you is connecting with a nonprofit microlender. A microlender is an organization that gives business loans to individuals. They typically charge higher-than-average interest rates and their maximum loan amount is usually $25,000.

Another option, if you are comfortable with it, is credit cards. This can be a great asset your company. What I do is charge everything to a cash back credit card. At the end of the month, take that cash and pay off the credit card statement with it. It is a nice little bonus each month. This will only work if you actually pay off the credit card each month. Otherwise, you can really get in trouble with credit card debt and pay high interest rates. The other option is to take the money and put it back into the business. Don't take it and put it in your personal accounts or use the points for a personal vacation. The business benefits should stay in the business.

One thing people forget to think about is how they will accept money, and if the bank or credit card is convenient for that. For example, do you have a physical store? Do you expect people to write you checks or accept cash? If so, you might want a bank that is close and convenient for you to deposit money. If you are an online business, does your bank have a user-friendly website? Can you do what you need to do with it?

Avoid Cash! Cash is so hard to keep track of and I personally don't like it when anyone uses it. Once a receipt is lost, it is hard to prove your purchase.

Credit Card Processors are another thing. Shop around for rates and convenience. Just because someone says that they can offer you credit card processing services does not mean they are the answer for you. Processors are offered by banks, accounting systems, and third parties. If you have a physical location, you would need a physical terminal. Which option gives you the best rates. If you are an online business, you won't need a physical terminal so choose one that doesn't offer that.

The last thing to think of is your accounting software. There are traditional desktop software programs and online programs. Think about your business again. If multiple people will be accessing the books, an online program might be more suitable. That way, the people who need access are looking at the most up to date version of the books and there is no overlapping work or hassle. This will allow you to avoid a large investment, only to figure out that you might change it. However, if you are a manufacturing or inventory heavy business you might need a desktop software. There are now online inventory systems that can handle retail stores, as well as integrate with your accounting system.

Make everything as simple as possible for yourself. It will benefit you if all your systems can talk to each other. You will have less work to do. When you are looking at how everything is going to work, having more systems is not necessarily better. Keep it simple. You don't have to change your systems every time something new is released. I had a client who did this very often and it was very frustrating for everyone. There was no continuity. You will be constantly re-inventing the wheel to make life easier. It will be hard to keep up. Change is good, keep it useful. The more time you spend on menial tasks, the less time you have for something that can make you money.

Learn to Delegate

I know you are a new business owner, and you are watching the bottom line. The other thing to consider is you don't have time to do it all yourself. Delegate as much as possible. Free up your time to sell your business and bring in new customers. If you do it all yourself, then you personally become the bottleneck and the reason your business isn't growing very well. I have made this mistake in the past. I was too concerned with paying my personal bills, I worked too much in the business and not on the business. Wrong Move! It almost caused the destruction of the thing I was trying so desperately to build. You should not start a business until you have money for yourself to live off of for two years. That isn't what I did, but I agree with it.

I found that people who work for small businesses and startups want to work. They will find ways to keep busy during the day or new ways to do things. They want to feel like they are a part of something. Make them feel like they are a part of something, even if you don't think you can fill their day with work. You will soon find that they are busy and able to either bring in more money or free up your time so that you can bring in more money. You may think that you are the master of all trades. Sorry, you are not. There is someone out there that can do your everyday tasks faster, cheaper, easier than you. Don't use so much of your own time, delegate.

I see everything in the business through the eyes of an Accountant. You should know the financial aspect of your business very well. The better you understand your financial position, the better business decisions you can make, and the more you can grow.

Let me give you a little accounting background. First off, there are a couple of different accounting methods. The most common methods are Cash and Accrual. Cash means that money comes in and out of your business. You don't owe or own anything and no one owes you. This applies to very little businesses. Otherwise, you would use Accrual which does keep track of bills you owe or people who owe you money. Even if your CPA files your taxes in the cash basis, you can still keep your day to day books in the accrual method. This is normal.

CPA Vs. Bookkeeper Vs Office Assistant

A bookkeeper takes care of the day to day accounting tasks and financial requirements. They provide documents to the CPA. A bookkeeper should have some accounting degree or certification in this field.

The CPA takes the information from the bookkeeper and fills out the end of the year taxes (or quarterly if applicable).

Office assistants are able to keep the books, but may not have the accounting, financial requirements or knowledge of the field. They may not fully understand the financials of the business. They may not be able to analyze the books or keep them "clean." They may not be properly communicating to the CPA or taking advantage of all the tax categories; for example, self-employed health care for an S-Corp vs. C-Corp.

Bank Statements should not be relied upon for financial information. The IRS requires that supporting documents are provided for any transaction in the business. This includes what was purchased, when and why. To provide this you must be able to produce business receipts. Bank statements are not sufficient. The vendor's name must be on the receipts. Banks tend to shorten or adjust the names. Also, the business reason for a transaction will be stated on an itemized receipt. This is why downloading or using automated accounting systems currently fail. For example, at Wal-Mart, you can purchase both ink and your kid's bathing suit for $39.99. You will be unable to prove that the purchase has anything to do with the business by using a bank statement. They also need to know the amount.

Humans make errors, so it is important to check the amount charged. For example, think about a restaurant check, you have to hand write a tip, then the server needs to enter it correctly. That is two interactions with humans that can create errors. Bank statements are still very important to reconcile the register. They ensure that the correct amount was charged or entered. This will also help determine what still has to come through for cash flow purposes.

# Things You Own

The Balance sheet is an important statement for your business. It shows the things that you own and the things you owe. This section is about the things you own.

The assets of the business are what the business owns. The assets section holds the balances of any bank accounts that you have; how much money you can spend (not that you should). This also holds the value (cost) of any inventory that you own, if applicable.

It also shows the balance of any Accounts Receivable. This is the amount of money that others owe you. I suggest that as a business, if your clients/customers pay you later, that you have a policy in place to collect on this. Do not be afraid to call or email to collect on this money. Some people add interest to late payments. You can do this if you make the customer is aware of this upfront. There is bound to be some people you can't collect from. In this case, you can move the amount to an expense account. Do not delete the invoice or trail that shows that the person owes you money. When I write off accounts, I look at how much and why. This way you can identify if there is a pattern, for example, a type of customer or a particular service. You can use that information to adjust your business. Maybe that type of customer shouldn't be a customer of yours anymore.

The cost of your inventory, if you have any, will be located here. It will be at a cost to you to purchase the inventory for resale. One thing to note is that every year you must take a physical inventory count of everything that you own for tax purposes to make sure that the account balance is correct. This will also facilitate removing any spillage from the account. Spillage is anything that has been lost, damaged or stolen.

The most common deposit that may be required for you to provide personally for a service, is a security deposit for renting a physical location. If you don't have the security deposit or a physical location don't worry. If you run everything out of a home office, for tax reasons, a different method is used. There are no expenses or anything that is associated with your personal house that goes through the books.

This area also shows any buildings, equipment or vehicles that your business owns. Each year, these accounts will decrease based on value until they are zero or sold off and removed from the books.

When I first started, after reading all the books, I went a little buy-crazy. I bought the big computer, the nice desk, the desktop software. Why? Because that is how I thought businesses are run. That is what is needed. Well, needless to say, it was all a waste. I currently just use a laptop and I am usually on my porch outside. The other thing I was constantly told is to get an office so that people can find me. Well, I didn't do that either. It was just me at the time. I did find a co-working space and rented a desk. A much more reasonable thing for a new business.

If your business owns a vehicle that is used strictly for business purposes you may be able to deduct the vehicle. You must have a wrap on the vehicle, use it primarily for business and have a separate personal vehicle. However, business insurance taxes may apply. These insurance taxes may also fall at a higher rate. If you do choose to use a business vehicle, decide who will be the designated driver(s) ahead of time. It's useful to let the employees access a business vehicle for resourceful time and management purposes. However, insurance rates will increase when you add an additional party.

If you drive your personal vehicle for business reasons, you may be eligible for a deduction on your taxes. This possible deduction includes $0.535 off every mile driven for business purposes only (as of 2018). Make sure to keep track of the mileage in order to receive a discount. There are very simple phone apps that can help you with this. If you do choose to use a personal vehicle for work, it will not be represented in the financial statement or the assets of the business. Since the vehicle is owned by you and not the business, it will not be an asset to the business. The personal vehicle will be your own separate responsibility.

## Things You Owe

This section of the balance sheet represents the things that you owe or liabilities.

This is money you owe people. Here you will have your accounts payable. Accounts payable are any bills that are received and have not yet been paid. These should be the first things to be paid on time. You want to keep your vendors happy so that you can continue to run as a business.

Other business loans, credit cards, credit lines and mortgages are here. These are typically a fixed monthly fee at a set interest rate. If there is extra money in the business, first pay off the Account Payables, then the Credit Cards, then the other loans. The other loans should be paid off in the order of the highest interest rate first. It is ok to have some loans or debt in the business. However, just remember that interest is paid on the debt. Keep the debt as low as possible. I always recommend trying to pay at least twice the minimum monthly payments.

Sales taxes are the taxes paid to the state each month based on your sales. Each state is slightly different in what and how much tax is collected. The general rule of thumb is that sales taxes are collected on any physical item sold to an end user. Sales taxes are paid by the customer, held by the company, and paid out of the company at the end of the month. This is not an expense to the business since it is paid by the customer, but it is held and paid by the business.

Payroll and Payroll Taxes to be paid later is found in this Book.

Equity Section

This section is the catch-all for the business. The most important part is the Owner / Member Contributions / Draws. This is the money that you have put into or taken out of the business (unless you pay yourself on payroll). Don't worry about the other accounts in the equity section.

# Income

This is the most important thing in your business. It keeps you open and going every day. So where does your income come from? Ultimately, you want income to continue to come into your business.

What does that income look like for you? Do you provide a service or a product?

If you provide a service, is it recurring? Recurring services means that you will get money in the future as well. This can be maintenance or a recurring appointment. If it is recurring, there are many programs out there that once the invoice is entered, it can email your clients within the designated time frame. You can even automatically charge your clients each time frame or have them put in their credit cards themselves. These simple steps will save you time as your business grows, so start them now. That way you are not overwhelmed or too busy later. As a small business owner, you will be too busy.

If you sell products, do you have an inventory system? The inventory systems do not necessarily have to feed into your accounting system. These can be very expensive and may not be necessary. Any bookkeeper worth their salt can use journal entries to put the correct amounts in the books from your inventory system.

Here is something to think about, if you have two business segments. Say, for example, you provide set up service and a maintenance service to your customers. Create two different income accounts for these services. This will allow you to see a little down the road where your money is coming from. Then you can focus on that and grow your business. Don't create an account for everything that you provide, but two or three accounts will allow you to see different things that bring in money without being overwhelming.

# Cost of Goods Sold

If you sell products you will have Cost of Goods Sold accounts. This is the cost of the product that you paid for it and then sold to your customer. Retail stores will sometimes try to assign a cost of the goods value for the labor provided for something. Unless you are a manufacturing business, the cost of your people will not go here. If you do put a cost of goods sold for labor in your inventory system, it can skew the numbers and be incorrect.

If you do have a couple of different income accounts, I would create matching Cost of Goods Sold accounts. That way you can easily see how much of a margin you have in each income segment. For example, if you have income accounts ABC, DEF, and GHI then you would have Cost of Goods Sold Accounts ABC, DEF, and GHI. It will make it easier for you to view and see your business. Ultimately seeing where you make money, and where you should focus your attention.

# Expenses

Expenses can make or break a company. This is what you spend your money on, or how much it takes you to run your business on a day to day basis. Spend the money. If you don't, you will never grow, but at the same time spend wisely.

Before I dive into Expenses, I want to tell you about expenses in general. There are two types of expenses; fixed and variable. Examples of fixed expenses are rent, website, or maybe phone. No matter how much or how little you make, you will have to pay for these items. Variable items are items that increase the amount of income you make. For example, as your business grows (more income) you will most likely hire employees, so your payroll expense will increase.

This is very important in a business because of the breakeven point. This is the amount of income you have to bring in to make money. Your income has to at least cover the number of fixed expenses that you have. Your net income (the amount you would take home) is the amount of additional income that you have, minus the variable expenses. You can budget and have projections but you will never really know until you start your business. If your business doesn't surpass the breakeven point, you will not make enough to survive.

As a business owner, you should have enough money to support yourself for two years prior to taking a salary from your company. For most of us, that is just not going to happen, which leads to slower business growth. You can't only spend the money on expenses, or you might become your own bottleneck to your company.

Advertising

This is a very interesting area. There are a lot of different advertising and media outlets these days. The average person will contact your business after hearing about it 3 times, so you must get your message out in different ways. Be aware that most advertising comes with a contract, so be sure to read it for future expenses.

When I started my business, everyone said if I wanted more clients, I should advertise in the Yellow Pages. So I did. But when I thought about it, I couldn't remember the last time I saw a Yellow Pages. If I am searching for something online, I will probably not go for Yellow Pages. I'm not saying that it won't work for your business, but it didn't for mine. This is your business, think about your clients, where do you go to look for something? Where are your clients?

Google Ad-words are great if you have a large adverting budget. They work by using the keywords that you choose to attach to your ad. If these keywords are typed into a search, then your ad will appear. If you outbid everyone else in front of you, your ad will appear at the top. Only the top couple of companies actually show up. Give it some careful thought. Do you click on Google Ads?

These can be useful for getting the word out about your business. Think about your customers, who they are and what appeals to them.

Where are your customers? If you were looking for your business, what would you do? Where would you go?

Bad Debt Expense

This is an interesting account, where you put all the invoices (accrual method only) that you do not expect to collect income on. I do recommend paying attention to this account as well as your receivables. You work for your money and you need to be paid. This is the money that isn't being collected. Look at why it isn't collected? Can you adjust a part of your business to avoid this?

Bank Service Charges

Depending on your bank they might charge you monthly service charges if you don't meet certain requirements. If you know those requirements, you can very easily avoid these fees. These fees can easily be $20 a month, equals to $240 in annual savings by knowing the minimum requirements. This is where overdraft fees are. Overdraft fees are very easy to avoid if your business books are kept up to date. You will be able to see how much money is in the bank and what checks still have not cleared. Pay attention to both to avoid overdraft fees. These service charges can be avoided easily. This can be a big expense for a new business.

Charitable Contributions

This is the value of goods or money that you give to charity. The charity in return should give you a paper stating that they are a charitable organization and their status and number with the government. Unfortunately, your time is not a charitable contribution. While it is great that you volunteer to help, you cannot deduct it on your taxes or books.

Insurance

The business should carry general business insurance. Depending on how many employees (doesn't matter if they are part or full time) your state might also require workers' compensation insurance. Insurance is there to protect your business in case you are sued. These options should be discussed with an insurance agent or lawyer depending on your business and legal business structure.

## Health Insurance

You do not have to offer health insurance to your employees if you have less than 50 (as of 2016). If you are self-employed, you can have the business pay your health insurance. You may be taxed on the value of the premiums paid through the business, but this depends on the business structure. That being said, the business can't pay for any co-pays, medicine or any other items. If you offer health insurance or any other benefit to any of your employees, you have to offer it to all of them.

## Interest Expense

This is the amount of money you pay to borrow any money that you have, for example, the interest on any credit line or loan. Keep this as low as possible because it is just throwing money out of your business. This should not be a large portion of the expenses in the business, even though many businesses do have loans or need capital to get started, or to grow. Please be smart about how to spend your money. This account has crushed businesses because they were overwhelmed or didn't know what to pay first or how the flow of money works. The general rule of thumb is to pay off items that have a hard due date (electric bill), then pay off items that cost the most (credit cards), then go down to everything else.

Internet Services

This includes everything from subscriptions to your website and the use of social media. As a business, you should own the domain for your business name. Your business name should be the website, email, business card and social media name. The more consistency in the business and name recognition the better. If anyone hears about your business they can easily find or contact you on whatever media they are using. This is fairly inexpensive to set up. Be careful and shop around. Some website design places or IT places will offer to host your email for much more money and you might not get any more benefit from it. Just know your options. Make sure your social media, website and email matches. I do know people who will not contact a business because they use "@gmail.com" or @yahoo.com". They assume they are not a real business.

Websites are not very hard to create. There are services out there like Weebly or Squarespace that allow you to create your own website for very little money. If you want a customized website, feel free to use the necessary resources. You can find web designers on freelance sites, for example, upwork.com. However, I do have many clients who pay hundreds of dollars for a custom HTML site when one of the free services looks just as good, or have it changed later

Visiting your homepage is likely to be the first experience one has with your business, so it shouldn't be too difficult to see why it is one of the most important pages of your website. Your homepage will receive the vast majority of traffic, and since first impressions are always very important, it is essential that you get it just right. The goal of your homepage and any landing pages is to turn as many of your first-time visitors into paying customers. Here are several key elements that your homepage should have in order to increase its conversion rate:

- Your Company Logo
- Engaging Headlines
- An Introduction
- Testimonials
- Navigation
- Images or Videos

Marketing / Social Media

If you are not a social media person there are services out there that can do it for you.

Marketing services also exist to make sure that your page shows up at the top of search engines and to maintain your social presence. According to the American Marketing Association, "Marketing is the activity, set of institutions, and processes for creating, communicating, delivering, and exchanging offerings that have value for customers, clients, partners, and society at large." No matter how successful your business, you need to keep the customers you have and attract new ones. As an entrepreneur, you must spend a majority of your time running the business and making sure the highest quality products and services are being provided. Effective marketing is a key component of success but implementing a marketing campaign can pose many challenges for the uninitiated. Do your research into the company and your options. These can be very expensive. While marketing itself is very hard to prove an actual return in customers or new customers, there is nothing worse than paying a lot of money for something that you either feel you could have done or didn't provide many benefits.

There are many programs and subscriptions out there that you can subscribe to. There is one for everything. Keep in mind that these subscriptions and programs are meant to make your life easier. A lot of these will interact with each other. If you have to click three buttons, there can be a simpler way. I had a client who would get so excited about all of these new programs and new things on the internet. He was constantly changing programs and processes in his business to make things easier and more efficient. There was a problem with this: 1) his employees had a hard time keeping up with everything 2) the constant changes didn't give any one system a chance to see if it was actually working. The purpose was defeated.

Meals and Entertainment

Meals and Entertainment is an account I hear a lot of interesting things about. This account is for the purchase of any meal or entertainment with a potential client or with the purpose of growing your business. It is not your daily meals or groceries. Only 50% of this account is written off on your taxes.

It is not that each dollar is returned to you or written off. When something is tax deductible, a portion of it is taken off your taxes. Then that final number is multiplied by your tax rate. A simple example is a $50 meal. You can write off $25. Of the $25, say you are in the 22% tax bracket, you only actually take off $5.50 of the $50 that was just spent.

Professional Fees

This includes any contractor or professional you pay throughout the year. Every small business should have a lawyer, Accountant, and CPA in this category. Other things you might find here is business coaches or consulting fees. Like marketing professionals, with the coaches and consultants, you want to make sure you are getting your money's worth. Ask around for recommendations. One thing I spent my money on was a staffing agency. Staffing agencies take a percentage of the yearly salary of whomever it is they are hiring for you. They do have access and accounts with job recruiting companies like Monster or Indeed to get the job posting out farther than you could on your own.

Rent and Utilities

This is also a fun section that has recently changed in the rulebooks. If you have a traditional brick and mortar business or office, this probably doesn't apply to you. A lot of things I hear is about the home-based business. To get a home business deduction, you cannot have a second office. Your office has to be separate from the rest of the house and cannot have a TV in it (I know weird). On your tax return, not in the books, you can take the square footage of the home and apply a percentage to it for the deduction. You cannot run your electric or cable bills for your house through the business

## Cash Flow

The only thing you really need to know is the amount of actual cash increase or decrease over a period of time in your business.

If you talk to any small-business owner, the biggest challenge he or she faces on a regular basis is cash flow. Managing cash flow is a constant struggle for many business owners, and the success or failure of their business frequently rides on it. Many small business owners don't want to deal with the cash flow topic because they think it's all about numbers, but it's actually more about the health of your business. Simply stated, you need to make sure you have more cash coming in than you have going out. You should know what your cash flow looks like and have the ability to change it when needed and know what action to take to improve the situation. Below are a few tips to consider to help manage your cash flow.

## Increase the Amount of Cash Coming In

You can raise your prices. This is one of the toughest things for small-business owners to do. Many fear that if they raise prices all the customers will stop buying from them. Luckily, that normally doesn't happen. Sure, you may lose a few customers, but they would have walked away at some point anyway. You want customers who value what you sell and appreciate their relationship with your company.

You can change payment terms. If your business model is such that you do the work and then invoice to get paid, it's time to shake that up. Set and enforce rules for getting paid within a shorter time frame. Most service providers allow a 30-day payment term, meaning you aren't getting paid until 45 or 60 days after your work is complete. Shorten your terms to 5 to 10 days, make sure you invoice right away and put a due date on the invoice. Use an online invoicing service so you don't have a time lag. You could also consider collecting partial payment at the start of the work, and the balance when it's complete. This is your business and you can set the rules any way you like.

You can capitalize on your success. Find your bestselling items, then examine what part of your target market is buying those items and concentrate your marketing efforts on selling more to that market. Many small-business owners are in the habit of coming up with new ideas or creating new things to sell. That's not bad, but it often results in the products or services that are a success to get put on the back burner, when they could be bringing much needed cash into your business.

## Decrease the Amount of Cash Going Out

You can leverage payment practices. You want to stretch out paying your bills for as long as possible. Set up a schedule of payments for your current bills and don't pay them until they are due. There is no need to put that cash in another business until it's required. And if the company accepts credit cards, use them to pay your bills, giving you another 20 to 30 days before the cash has to leave your business. Be sure to manage it so you don't incur fees and end up with long-standing debt.

You can renegotiate fees with vendors. If you have recurring bills; for example, phone, internet, office space and fees with other vendors, review each agreement and determine whether there's a way to lower your regular payment. Things are always changing, and, as technology improves, many services become less expensive. Nothing will change unless you ask.

You can adjust inventory levels. If your business must keep inventory on hand, take a good look at your records to see if there are items that could be reduced or ordered less frequently. Inventory on hand will cost your business money. You might also want to consider if drop shipping would work for your business so you don't have to manage inventory at all.

If you're in a cash flow crunch, try some or all of these tips to help dig you out. This is by no means a comprehensive list of things you can do, but it will get you started.

## Employees and Payroll Taxes

How you pay yourself is determined by the structure of your business. Generally, if you have a sole-proprietorship or a partnership, you would take money out of the business through a "draw" account. In this scenario, you would simply transfer the money to yourself. Then the self-employment taxes and the business funds are passed through to your own personal tax statement. On the other hand, you could pay yourself as an employee if you have a corporation because the business is considered an entity separate from yourself. These are the general rules, but there can be other position designations for your business.

Independent Contractors Vs. Employees

This depends on a lot of different factors. If they work under their own business name and work for more than one person, they are an independent contractor and will receive a Form 1099 at the end of the year. Otherwise, they are an employee and must have employment taxes taken out of their pay. If you are not sure, you can file a Form SS-8 with the IRS and they will make the determination.

Form 1099

A Form 1099 is a form that the IRS uses for information purposes. You have to file a Form 1099-MISC for any payments for services over $600.

If you have been paying an independent contractor, that is an employee or vice versa; there are resources available to you by the IRS. This would have to be handled by your own state and local revenue department based on state and local employment taxes. Either way, it is an issue that should be remediated as soon as possible to avoid further possible taxes and penalties.

Employee handbook

Employee handbooks are a good idea for any business environment, although one is not needed. They can set out a clear explanation about the policies of your business and what is expected if policies are not followed. What is included in an employee handbook is up to you, but the following are some suggestions:

- Work hours /Schedules
- Code of Conduct
- Benefits (both required and optional)
- Leave policies

Employee Documents

Certain documents must be completed to hire a new employee. They are required to be kept in perpetuity. The federal government required the following documentation:

- Social Security Card – Check for accuracy
- Form W-4 – Employee's Withholding Allowance Certificate
- Form I-9 – USCIS Employment Eligibility Verification
- States may also require additional documentation or require reporting of hiring to the state of employment. View your state Revenue or Labor department for this information.

Additional Documents can be required for a business to keep regarding an employee varies by the type of business being conducted. These requirements are based on the laws that apply to your business.

Be sure to check with the department of labor in your state for any additional requirements.

Types of Taxes

Depending on the type of business, you have to pay the following types of taxes:

- Income Tax
- Self-employment taxes
- Excise tax
- Payroll taxes: Unemployment, Withholding

Federal taxes are due quarterly or yearly. This information is found on your federal EIN statement. The state business taxes can be found at your state revenue department.

# About the Author

Kaylin is the owner and founder of Bean Counters Bookkeeping. Her interest in small businesses began in college while working for a successful small business called Bike Cycles in Wilmington, North Carolina. There she received hands on training in business management and came face to face with the daily challenges of a small business.

After completing her Masters of Science in Accountancy at the University of North Carolina Wilmington, she worked for the U.S. Army Audit Agency for over three years. It was here she learned the methods of detailed accounting and auditing. After working for the government, Kaylin discovered her interest in small businesses was not fulfilled and there was a burning desire within to become an entrepreneur.